A Stroll Through the Centuries:

150 Years of Images of Chagrin Falls, Ohio

Chagrin Falls Historical Society

Laura J. Gorretta, Editor

Chagrin Falls Historical Society Press – 2017

Foreword

One of my favorite things to do at the museum is to browse through our extensive collection of photographs. We have scanned over 7000 photographs and glass plate negatives to date. They tell an interesting story about how a village developed and prospered, through good times and bad.

Chagrin Falls was home to a number of early photographers. Most prominent among them were Thomas Shaw and E. R. Higbee. Shaw and Higbee produced a series of stereographs of scenes around the village in the 1870s and 1880s. The glass plate negatives they used survived and are in our collection.

At a young age, Austin H. Church, the son of Henry Church Jr., began working with Thomas Shaw learning the art of photography. Church took photographs throughout the Chagrin Valley of a variety of businesses, family gatherings, prominent people and events – and it is from his work that the glass plates were passed down through the family and are now included in our collection. As negatives transitioned from glass to celluloid, and photography became more available to the average citizen, Church began using the new Kodak camera. We have boxes of these negatives that we still have to process.

If you find the photographs in this book interesting, find some time to stop by the museum and 'rummage' through our collections – it's my favorite thing to do.

John Bourisseau, President
Chagrin Falls Historical Society

Visit our web site – **chaghist.org**
Find us on

Table of Contents

Preface V

Acknowledgments VII

Aerial View of Downtown 2-3

Grove Hill 4

West Orange Street 7

Cleveland Street Bridges 9

East Orange Street 11

North Main Street (East Side) 12

Bell Street 16

North Main Street 22

East Washington Street 32

South Main Street 38

East Washington Street 40

South Franklin Street 42

West Washington Street (from Triangle Park) 45

Triangle Park 49

North Franklin Street 51

North Main Street (West Side) 56

Phoenix Block 59

River Street 61

West Street 63

North Main Street 65

Additional Chagrin Falls Historical Society publications available for purchase 70

Preface

When Noah Graves first stumbled upon the High Falls in 1833 he immediately envisioned a manufacturing community similar to those he left behind in his native Massachusetts. Water power meant mills and mills meant manufacturing. Although others had settled along the river in isolated cabins, and there was a sawmill on the river in operation when Graves arrived, he recognized the potential for a thriving community built among the hilly, heavily forested and often swampy area along the river. The villagers settled on both sides of the line separating Cuyahoga and Geauga Counties, an inconvenience that was solved when the Ohio Legislature approved a plan to annex land in Geauga County to Cuyahoga County in 1841. This move resulted in the bump into Geauga County where Chagrin Falls is situated on the map, interrupting an otherwise straight county line.

By 1842, the village map looked very much as it does today. Some of the street names have changed; Pearl Street is now West Washington Street and Front Street is now Bell Street. West Cottage Street was not a dead end. Sophia Street was planned, but never developed. But those changes are minor. We have arranged this book as if you are walking through the village beginning and ending at Grove Hill, venturing down the side streets as you go. Image selection was difficult; we have over 7000 scanned images in our collection but we believe we have chosen images that will give you a good idea of what Chagrin was like not so very long ago. If you have been away from Chagrin Falls for a long time, you will recognize the place. If you are new to Chagrin, what came before will look familiar to you.

We were eager to add a photographic tour of the village to our growing list of publications. If you would like additional information about the people, buildings or events mentioned in this book, please consult our other publications or come to the Historical Society to peruse our extensive research collection.

Acknowledgments

The Publications Committee worked together to produce a book which would give the reader an idea through photographs taken or images drawn dating back over a 150 years of how the village of Chagrin Falls has evolved. All the photographic images in this book are from the Historical Society Collections. Some have been added recently. The task of selecting the photos for inclusion was taken on by Laura Gorretta and Laurie Loveman. When a current photograph was needed to illustrate a particular change – or lack of change – the Committee turned to member and photographer Terence T. Blair to find the right vantage point on a sunny day. Photographs taken by Society President John Bourisseau in 2008 are included, as well.

But a book of photographs without a little history to supply context isn't particularly useful. Laura Gorretta and Laurie Loveman used the Society's research materials to provide accurate text for the photos. Laurie's experience as an author makes her invaluable as an editor. Committee member Don Barriball confirmed dates and events. Special thanks go to Museum Curator Pat Zalba, Museum Director Jane Babinsky and Photo Archivist Zo Sykora.

Pulling it all together was Committee member and graphic designer Bill Reid of re:id Design + Direction, whose creative layout of the photographs and the cover design make this publication special.

A project such as this requires many more volunteer hours than you might expect in order to "get it right." We are confident this book was worth the wait.

Chagrin Falls Historical Society
Publications Committee
Laura Gorretta, Chair

March 2017

2 A Stroll Through the Centuries

Aerial photograph of downtown Chagrin Falls, circa 1957, showing North Main Street and the area from Bell Street to East Washington Street prior to the building of the shopping plaza in 1963. Pleasant Alley was a residential street before the shopping center was built.

Grove Hill

Looking southeast from the top of Grove Hill, showing the building at 98 North Main Street (now Huntington Bank) that was built in 1846 and is the oldest commercial building on North Main Street. Also visible are three brick buildings constructed with common walls, the tallest of which was built in 1857. Next, is the Chagrin Falls Paper Mill and Sack factory with its tall chimney, the Main Street bridge and the Mechanics Row which continued up Bell Street.

A slightly different view showing the west side of North Main Street. This image was taken between 1867 and 1875 before the second story and cupola were added to Township Hall. The steeple of the Methodist Church on the east side of South Franklin Street, built in 1846, can be seen right of center.

This view, ca. 1910, shows the south end of Henshaw Nursery on Grove Hill with Main Street visible left of center. Township Hall, with its cupola, is in the center. The homes in the foreground are on West Cottage Street.

Looking from West Cottage Street toward North Main Street, ca. 1955. The spire of the Federated Church on Bell Street can be seen in the center. The cupola of the school on Philomethian Street is to the right of the spire. The two story wooden building on Main Street was constructed ca. 1845 and is still in use today.

A Stroll Through the Centuries

The Bayard Tavern was built in 1835 at the foot of Grove Hill. In the 1840s it was a stage coach stop on the road from Cleveland to Warren. This woodcut was made by Jehu Brainerd in the 1840s.

The Bayard Tavern was also known at various times as the Union House and the Colby House. The building was torn down in 1925 to make room for Spaller's Gas Station.

Chagrin Falls Historical Society 7

Walt Spaller's Fleetwing Gas Station and Jim Bowe's Lunchroom were at the corner of West Orange and North Main Streets in the 1920s.

West Orange Street

West Orange Street looking west ca. 1880.

West Orange Street in 2017.

8 A Stroll Through the Centuries

In the early 1900s Chagrin Falls was home to six gas stations and as many car dealerships. The east side of Grove Hill at East Orange Street was at one time the site of a Gulf gas station and later a Chevrolet dealership. Ca. 1970.

The car dealership closed and Stepnorth took its place in the 1970s.

Cleveland St. Bridges

Originally a stone bridge constructed in 1853, in 1888 it was replaced by a "modern" iron bridge. The north end of the bridge was flanked by the buildings of the Adams Bag Company. The Adams Bag Company and its successors, the Chase Bag Company and later, IVEX, operated the mill for over 100 years and was a major village employer. Note the wagon tracks heading up the hill. Cleveland Street originally cut up the hill, across High Street and continued to meet Falls Road.

10   A Stroll Through the Centuries

The modern iron bridge gave way to a concrete bridge in 1914.

The Cleveland Street bridge in 2017. The ruins of the paper mill are visible on the left.

Chagrin Falls Historical Society 11

The village as seen from North Street rounding the curve onto East Cottage Street ca. 1870. The prominent building with the belfry atop, is the Congregational Church on East Orange Street. The house just left of the church was the home of William T. and Alice Upham which was moved to East Cottage Street when the Valley Lutheran Church was built. The houses on East Orange Street, the river, the buildings on Bell Street and the Chagrin Falls Paper Mill on North Main Street can be seen from this vantage point.

East Orange Street

East Orange Street ca. 1880. The Congregational Church bell tower is visible on the right.

This Italianate style building at 18 East Orange Street was built ca. 1870 for Joseph Stoneman and his family. Originally a residence, it has served as the headquarters for American Legion Post 393 and various retail establishments over the years.

North Main Street

East Side from East Orange to the Chagrin River

The Sassy Cat at 88 North Main in the 1970s was an arts and crafts consignment shop. The building was constructed ca. 1845 by Daniel Warren, founder of Warrensville Township, as a residence.

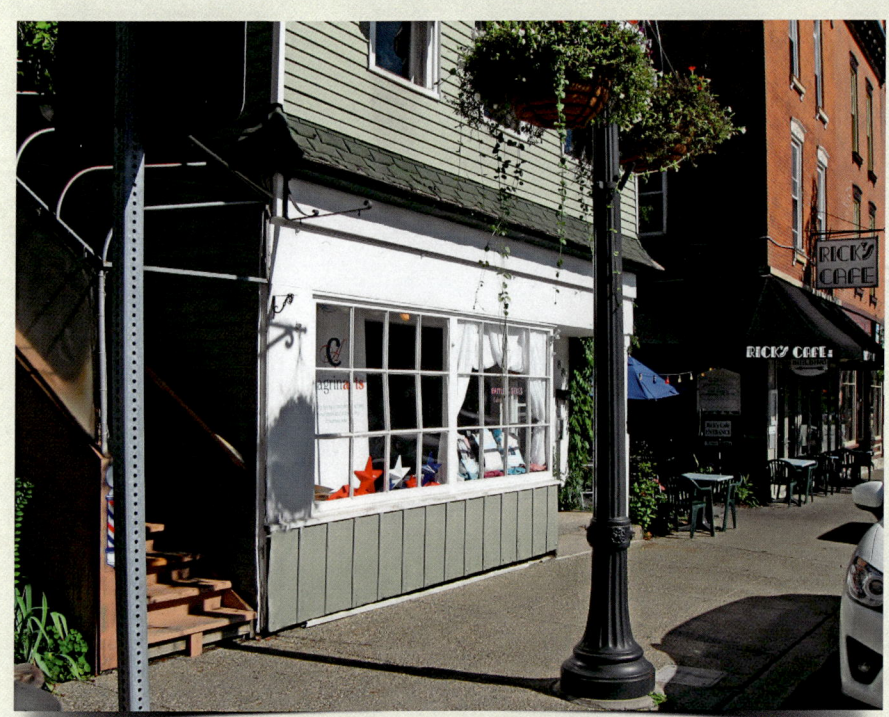

The building is the headquarters of Chagrin Arts in 2017.

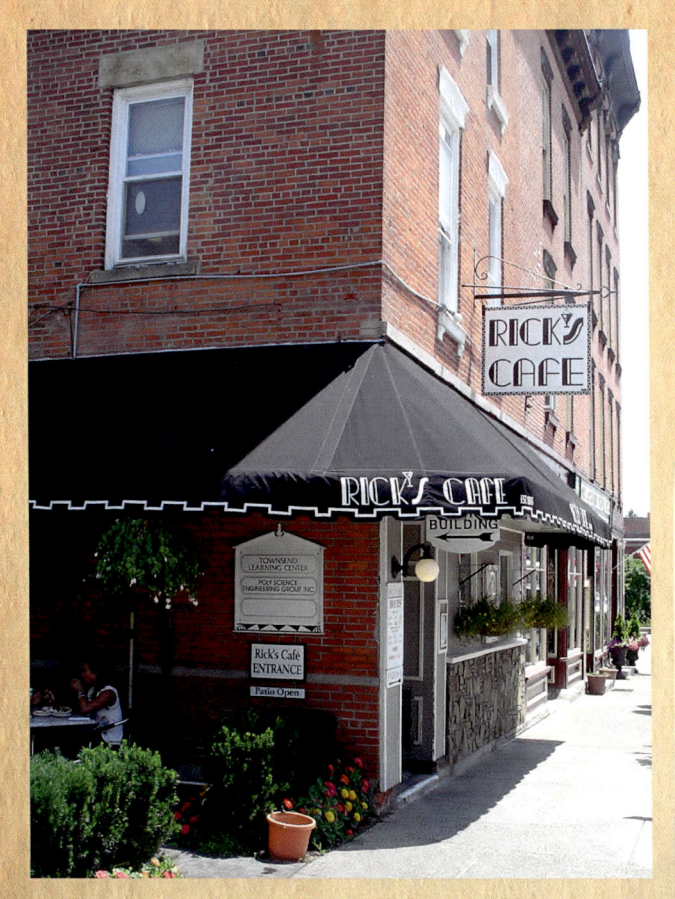

The Valley Tavern is now Rick's Cafe. The G.A.R. (Grand Army of the Republic) held its meetings on an upper floor of the building in the late 1800s and early 1900s. This building was the location at times of a tinware shop and hardware business as well as several restaurants over the years.

Chagrin Hardware Store and Masonic Hall in 1923. A hardware store has been operating in this building since 1857. In 1891 the Golden Gate Masonic Lodge added a floor to the building to serve its membership. The Wilbur P. Bowe Grocery Store is the building to the north.

Chagrin Falls Hardware Store in 2017.

14 A Stroll Through the Centuries

View of North Main Street, taken from the Main Street bridge looking north up Grove Hill in the early 1920s. The building which sat next to the Chagrin River was built in 1836 as the Chagrin Falls Paper Mill. These buildings were demolished in 1931 to make the entrance to Riverside Park.

Chagrin Falls Historical Society   15

In 1931 the Village passed a bond issue to demolish old buildings on North Main Street in order to create an entrance to Riverside Park. This view of the 1942 V-Day parade on North Main Street shows the entrance to the park. Buildings on East Orange Street are visible behind the Chagrin Hardware.

Entrance to Riverside Park in 2017.

16 A Stroll Through the Centuries

Bell Street

A pre-1880 photo of Bell Street, known at the time as Front Street, looking east on Bell from North Main Street. The shops on the left were known as "Mechanics Row" and housed a print shop, carriage shops, a blacksmith shop and, at one time, the Falls Café. The Free Will Baptist Church is in the background at the juncture of Vincent and Bell Streets. The R. Rowe & Son Carriage Shop and Russell & Bro. Cabinet & Chair Factory are on the left.

Bell Street and the Bell Street Park from North Main Street in 2017.

The wooden buildings of Mechanics Row are vacant in this ca. 1912 photo. In 1914 the abandoned buildings were torn down. The land formerly occupied is now the Bell Street Park.

Falls Implement Company and Buckeye Laundry occupied 23 Bell Street ca. 1915. It was originally the site of the Chagrin Falls Creamery and in the 1920s became the home of the Hessey Hatchery and later, Chuck's Beverage. In 2017, Chuck's Fine Wines occupies the building.

18   A Stroll Through the Centuries

The building at 15 Bell Street was originally a wagon shop before it became Weller's blacksmith shop in the late 1800s.

Looking east from the Main Street bridge toward the dam in this pre-1914 photo. The dam supplied power for a sawmill and for the Chagrin Falls Paper Company which was located where the entrance to Riverside Park is today. The overhanging attachment to the blacksmith shop is the outhouse.

The same view in 2017.

Chagrin Falls Historical Society 19

Bell Street looking east near Philomethian Street. The brick building on the right is the Enterprise Flouring Mill built by William Hutchings and Benajah Williams, Jr. in 1879. It burned in 1965. Beyond are the Ober Manufacturing Company buildings ca. 1881.

Buildings along the north side of Bell Street in 2017. The two story frame building was the location of Greenaway's Grocery. The Valley Art Center completes the block.

20　A Stroll Through the Centuries

A view of the railroad yard and the extensive Ober Manufacturing complex taken from the school on Philomethian Street. The pasture at the top of the photo is the site of Hamlet Retirement Village.

The little white building behind the trains was the office for the company and next to it is one of the factory buildings.

The only remaining buildings from the Ober Manufacturing Company in 2017.

The Federated Church resulted from the combination of the Disciples of Christ Church and the Congregational Church which had separate church buildings in the village. The western portion of this building was constructed in 1875 and remodeled in 1885.

A new sanctuary and Fellowship Hall were added to the Federated Church in 1965.

North Main Street
East Side at Bell Street

This view shows the east side of North Main Street, taken after the stone bridge was built in 1858. The building with the second floor balcony, far right, is the Eggleston Hotel at the corner of North Main Street and East Washington Street.

The small dam visible at the bottom right corner of the image supplied water to run the water wheel at the grist mill located at the end of the bridge on Main Street. Excess water was used by S & H Earl's Woolen Mill on River Street.

Chagrin Falls Historical Society 23

North Main Street looking south from Bell Street in 1908. From left to right are the Ober Building. The Ober Building housed the Ober Furniture Store and Funeral Parlor. L. W. Wyckoff Jewelers and Opticians was also located in the Ober Building. A fire in 1963 destroyed the third floor of the Ober Building. The Bradley Building is just south of the Ober Building.

North Main Street in 2017.

24   A Stroll Through the Centuries

The Bradley store was originally a frame building that was replaced with a brick building in 1893. In 2017 it houses the Flip Side Restaurant.

The view in 1978 from the point of Triangle Park. The Wolf's Harness Shop Building dates back to 1874 and was the location of a harness shop until the 1980s. The bank building was constructed in 1962 at the entrance to the shopping center.

Chagrin Falls Historical Society 25

The Chagrin Falls Savings and Loan Company, ca. 1900. The Savings and Loan found new quarters south of Triangle Park in the 1920s. The building was moved to Hall Street in the 1930s. This location is next to the driveway into the shopping center.

The Kelley Wickoff Block of buildings is on the east side of North Main Street. The H.N. Wickoff Stoves & Tinware shop is on the right. Hiram H. Kelley operated a grocery and hardware business on the left. Photo ca. 1870.

The Chagrin Falls Fire Department and City Hall used the first and second floors of this building from 1897 to 1938 when the village offices moved to West Washington Street. The International Order of Odd Fellows (IOOF) occupied the third floor of both this building and the Kelley Building next door. This building dates back to 1888. This photo was taken in the 1930s.

This photo of North Main Street dates from the early 1900s. At the right is Vacker's Pharmacy in the Wickoff Building. The tracks of the Cleveland and Chagrin Falls Interurban railway which operated in Chagrin Falls from 1895 to 1925 can be seen in the foreground on East Washington Street.

Another view of North Main Street ca. 1900.

Automobiles line up across North Main Street for a race ca. 1920. The Harris Block next to the Wickoff Building was built for the Harris Brothers hardware store in 1911.

A Stroll Through the Centuries

East side of North Main Street ca. 1935, showing Central United National Bank. The Chagrin Falls Banking Company built this impressive building in 1923 and it has been the location of a bank since that time. The Chagrin Falls Post Office was located in a storefront until a Post Office building was constructed in the 1930s. A concrete traffic cone, known as a "deadman," directs cars to keep right with arrows pointing to Warren, Youngstown, Pittsburgh and to Cleveland. Before State Route 422 was rerouted south of Chagrin Falls, it was the primary road from Cleveland to Warren and beyond, entering the village on West Orange Street, continuing down North Main Street and out East Washington Street.

The view in 2017.

The Harris Block on the east side of North Main Street in the late 1970s.

East side of North Main Street in the late 1970s, showing Cameo Gift Shop, Evans Flowers, and Dink's Restaurant. Evans Flowers was located in the IOOF Building in the space once occupied by the fire department. Dink's was located in the Kelley Building.

The Irving House Hotel at the northeast corner of North Main and East Washington Streets. This photo was taken in the 1880s. A hotel or tavern house had been located at this corner since 1849. In the 1870s and 1880s it was a popular holiday location and businessman's hotel served by both the Interurban and the train that came into town further east on East Washington Street. The hotel burned to the ground on January 13, 1897. This land stood vacant until the 1920s.

Looking east from Triangle Park. The frame buildings on East Washington Street can be seen at the right.

This photo was taken from North Franklin Street across Triangle Park after the fire in 1897. The Cleveland & Chagrin Falls Interurban car is stopped on North Main Street in front of the ruins of the Irving House Hotel. The white building behind the ruins and facing East Washington Street was the livery stable for the hotel. When this photo was taken it was Mr. Joel Burnett's Livery and Feed Stable.

East Washington

The Interurban depot on East Washington Street ca.1918. From left to right are Motorman Steve Fortney, Conductor Bill Murtaugh and Tom Bennett. The Falls movie theater can be seen to the right.

View of the "picture show" building which later became the Falls Theater on East Washington Street. The building is festooned with flags and bunting for a holiday parade.

The Falls Theater was in operation from 1915 to 1979. This photo shows the Falls Theater just prior to demolition in 1979.

Harvey Chevrolet on East Washington Street in the 1960s was one of several car dealership in the village.

Built in 1955, this building served the community as the Curtiss Clinic until 1980 when the Clinic was moved further out East Washington Street. The Curtiss Clinic was named for Drs. Harvey and Paul Curtiss who cared for generations of residents. It was converted to an office building.

The façade of the 1914 high school building has not changed much in over 100 years.

George Ober built his home on East Washington Street in 1874. It became a funeral home in 1940, known to many as the Reed Nichols Funeral Home. In 2000 it was converted to an office building.

The Chagrin Falls Historical Society purchased the building in 2014 and launched a capital campaign to restore and renovate the building. It is the home of the Society's Museum and Sihler Research Center. The Bo Burr Community Room is available for use by community organizations.

36   A Stroll Through the Centuries

Railway transportation finally came to Chagrin Falls in 1877. The narrow gauge railroad that ran between Chagrin Falls and Solon carried passengers and freight. The yard extended from East Washington Street north to Bell Street.

143 East Washington Street, ca. 1962. This was the site of Elliott F. Shepard's feed store and the C & S Farmer's Exchange across the tracks. The feed store closed in 1963. After serving as a lumberyard, the building was taken over by Cleveland Plumbing Supply Company.

In 2017 the yard is the site of the Bell Tower Condominiums on Bell Street and this vacant lot.

The southeast corner of Main Street and East Washington Street ca. 1900. It was the location of the Continental Grocery store and the Wyckoff House restaurant. It was torn down to make way for a gas station.

The intersection in the early 1950s. The bowling alley on South Main Street also offered a popular lunch counter.

South Main Street

The Falls Hotel in 1898. The hotel opened in 1897 and featured furnace heat, electric lights, and a plumbing system which supplied hot and cold water throughout. A veranda was added in 1898 and a bathroom in 1899. The rate was $2.00 a day. It ceased being a hotel in the 1920s.

Chagrin Falls Historical Society 39

The Falls Hotel in 2017 is an office building.

The H.A. Sheffield & Son Monuments at 45 South Main Street in 1910. This is one of the oldest continuously operating businesses in the Village.

East Washington

The view up East Washington Street ca.1920. One Interurban car is headed up East Washington Street and one is headed down. The Interurban depot can be seen on the left.

East Washington Street looking east, ca 1930. Brewster and Stroud Company is located at the end of the block. The middle building was remodeled by the Chagrin Savings and Loan Company which moved there from its location on North Main Street. In 1929 the Harris Family replaced the frame building on the corner of South Franklin Street with the Harris-Gardner Building.

Chagrin Falls Historical Society   41

East Washington Street looking west ca. 1930.

East Washington Street looking west in 2017.

South Franklin Street

The Sheridan Building at 25 South Franklin Street. Fisher Foods Grocery Store occupied the first floor from 1939 to about 1962.

The Chagrin Falls Buick Co. ca. 1924.

Chagrin Falls Historical Society   43

The Methodist Church occupied a building on the eastside of South Franklin Street in the 1840s. The church moved across the street in 1885.

The Methodist Church ca. 1890.

The Church was expanded in 1950 with the addition of the two story Harris Hall. It was renovated again in 1980.

Henry Church, Jr.'s home and blacksmith shop on the southwest corner of Washington and South Franklin Streets. This photo was taken after 1897 when Church rented his blacksmith shop to Robert Gane. The sculpture in Church's front yard is the lion that now resides at his gravesite in Evergreen Hill Cemetery. The house was moved to Olive Street and the blacksmith shop was torn down to make way for the Masonic Hall in the 1920s.

The lion sculpture by Henry Church, Jr. marks his grave at Evergreen Hill Cemetery. It had been displayed at the Cleveland Museum of Art for many years. The sculpture was returned to the cemetery in 2014.

West Washington
from Triangle Park

The Golden Gate Lodge built the Masonic Hall at 1 West Washington Street in 1923. On the first floor are F. Bennett's Bakery (Chagrin Falls Home Bakery), A & P Grocery, Hughs Butcher Shop, and Standard Drug Store. The third floor is used for Masonic meetings and the second floor is a community room.

Masonic Hall ca. 1996. Harris Hall of the Methodist Church can be seen on the left.

This drawing of the house at 21 West Washington Street is from an 1874 Atlas of Cuyahoga County. The house was built in 1874 for Washington Gates, a village leader and entrepreneur. The property was purchased in 1938 by the Village of Chagrin Falls and continues to serve as the Village Hall. The bell tower of the Methodist Church on South Franklin Street is seen on the left.

A later view of
21 West Washington Street.

Chagrin Falls Village Hall at 21 West Washington Street. The third floor, which housed the village library and historical society was destroyed by a fire in January 1962. The cannon dates to the Civil War.

The Post Office at 34 West Washington Street was built in 1939 as a WPA (Works Progress Administration) project. Prior to the construction of this building, the Chagrin Falls Post Office occupied storefronts on North Main and North Franklin Streets. The Post Office was decommissioned when a new Post Office was built on East Washington Street in 1982.

Photo taken of the north side of West Washington Street. These men may have been linemen installing electrical lines for the interurban trains in ca. 1895.

Triangle Park

View of Triangle Park, ca. 1875. Henry Church, Sr. built his first house in Chagrin Falls in 1834. The house, seen on the west side of the Triangle, was moved to Hall Street in the 1880s to make room for a new building.

A view of Triangle Park ca. 1877. The Bandstand was originally topped off with deer antlers which can be seen in this photo. The saplings planted around the perimeter of the park were donated by village leaders.

50	A Stroll Through the Centuries

Triangle Park looking west at North Franklin ca. 1915.

Triangle Park in 2017.

North Franklin Street

1902 photograph of the Post Office at 11 North Franklin Street and Robens & Pelton Grocery Store. The postmen are ready to head out on their rounds.

52   A Stroll Through the Centuries

North Franklin Street ca. 1980. The corner building is frame and the next four buildings are brick and when built were known as the Park Block.

The south end of North Franklin Street in 2017.

North Franklin Street, ca. 1980,. Havre's is located in the McClentic building.

North Franklin Street showing the O.F. McClentic Company Dry Goods Store in the building McClentic built in 1882, the J.M. Gates Dry Goods Store and the Upham-Didham Clothiers.

54 A Stroll Through the Centuries

A similar view in 2017.

North Franklin Street in the 1870s showing W. H. Caley's Chagrin Falls Shoe Store

Chagrin Falls Historical Society 55

Tenny's Novelty Store and Millinery ca. 1907. H.D. Tenny bought the building containing three stores from J.M. Gates in 1884.

In 1910 H.D. Tenny tore down his frame building and built his new building at what is now 41 North Main Street.

North Main Street
East Side

Chagrin Falls Roller Mills on Main Street south of the Chagrin River, ca. 1920. The Tenny Building can be seen on the left.

A grist mill had been located at the top of the High Falls since 1836. In 1875 owner Washington Gates added the building north of the mill as an office and showroom. The mill changed hands several times over the years. In 1931, the Village purchased the mill to create a park to provide access to the river. The showroom was retained.

Chagrin Falls Historical Society 57

The Stairway to the Falls in 2017. The Stairway to the Falls is located between the Tenny Building and the Popcorn Shop. In 2003 an Ohio Bicentennial Historic Marker was placed at the top of the stairway to commemorate the importance of the High Falls.

58   A Stroll Through the Centuries

The Popcorn Shop in 2017.

Cyanotype of the High Falls dated between 1910 and 1914. Across the street is the Ober Building and a building that was part of Mechanic's Row on Bell Street. Note the dam at the base of the mill which supplied water power to the mill.

Phoenix Block

The Phoenix Block on the west side of North Main Street. This block of buildings originally comprised wooden structures that burned in 1868. Local builder William Hutchings purchased the property from the owners and built four separate buildings. The new buildings, like the mythical phoenix arose from the ashes. The back of the Tenny Building across the river can be seen in this image taken sometime after 1910.

60　A Stroll Through the Centuries

The Phoenix Block in 1983.

The Phoenix Block in 2017.

River Street

The Wren House at 9 River Street was built ca. 1872 as the Launspach Boot & Shoe Store. It was originally located at the corner of East Orange Street and North Main Street.

9 River Street in 2017.

Chagrin Valley Little Theatre at 40 River Street was constructed in 1949. It was the first permanent home of CVLT, which was founded in 1933. The Briggs Red Barn Antiques shop was housed in a barn that originally belonged to the house at 79 West Street.

The Chagrin Valley Little Theatre in 2017. In 2010 the Theatre acquired the Red Barn. The lobby and office areas of the Theatre were expanded in 2016.

West Street

The Village Exchange consignment shop at 79 West Street. In 2017 it is a restaurant operated by Gamekeeper's Taverne.

Exterior of Crane's Canary Cottage at 87 West Street. In 1927, Clarence Arthur Crane purchased two cottages on West Street. One was razed and an addition was joined to the Harvey Frost cottage to the north to create Crane's Canary Cottage. It gained a national reputation as a "delightful place for luncheon or dinner with superlative food served in a refined atmosphere." It closed at the beginning of World War II.

Gamekeeper's Taverne occupies the south end of the former Crane's Canary Cottage, 2008.

The entrance to the Inn of Chagrin Falls, 2008.

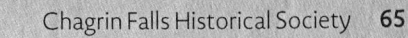

North Main Street

Chagrin Falls Township Hall on North Main Street ca. 1940.

Township Hall ca. 1975.

North Main Street in the 1880s. The building to the left of Township Hall was Tom Bradley's bakery which he opened in 1844. The Union House Hotel is at the corner of North Main Street and West Orange Street. The greenhouse for the Henshaw-Wyckoff nursery is also visible. The house at the top of Grove Hill has stood watch over the village since 1874.

A view of the west side of North Main Street showing the Phoenix Block and Township Hall ca. 1930. The village library was located on the second floor of the Phoenix Block.

William Stuck was the owner of this gas station in July, 1932 at the corner of North Main Street and West Orange Street. The station sold Canfield gas. Township Hall is in the background along with Shorts Ice Cream. This site has been the location for restaurants in recent years.

68 A Stroll Through the Centuries

The road down Grove Hill before it was paved.

The road down Grove Hill began as a narrow dirt track that was gradually widened to accommodate wagons and cars. In 1938, a little over 100 years later, the WPA straightened and paved the road and added a retaining wall.

Chagrin Falls Historical Society 69

Grove Hill ca. 2017.

Also Available

The following titles are also available for purchase through Chagrin Falls Historical Society Press. Look for them on our website, **chaghist.org** or at the Museum.

Chagrin Falls: An Ohio Village History, 2nd edition, 2014
Laura J. Gorretta, Editor

Mill Town on the Chagrin River: the History of the Early Mills and Foundries in Chagrin Falls, Ohio
By Don Barriball

The Stranahan Folding Canvas Boat Company
By Don Barriball

History of the Chagrin Hardware Company
By Don Barriball

The History of the Ober Manufacturing Company of Chagrin Falls
By Don Barriball

The History of the Cleveland & Chagrin Falls Interurban Railway
By Don Barriball

The Drawings of Max Barnard
Serapio R. Zalba, Editor

Annie's Anecdotes
By Anne Gumprecht

A Taste of the Past: From Our Fabulous Soups and Breads Luncheons
By Chagrin Falls Historical Society

Underground Railroads and Runaway Slaves in Early Chagrin Falls, Ohio
By Miriam Rose Church Stem
Jane Babinsky, Editor